For Mom

Dear Mom – Letters to Heaven

Looking back it seems so much longer now since Mom's been gone. When it's actually only been a year. What does that say about time? My wife and I were both shocked when we looked at her memoriam card and saw the date May 15, 2021. In speaking to my brother-in-law, friend and doctor he told us that typically a soul only lasts around five years in an assisted living facility until they pass. Mom thankfully skipped out after four. She didn't want to be there. Who does? But she got great care and was just down the street from family who visited her all the time. We loved her and even though my wife and I were several states away we would make the drive once every three months.

She told us on one visit that it was nice and then stopped herself and said it was "*damn* nice of you to take time out of your lives to come and visit me." First off mom did not have a foul mouth as is the trend these days and that got our attention. She was trying to let us know how sincere she was being. Message received. And second of all my wife and I responded with the emotion of "are you kidding me?" Both of us adored her and sought out her wisdom almost on a daily basis. She was a good hang! Another brother-in-law said to us when he heard she passed that she was a "Mom's mom." He nailed that one down right there. Not much more needed to be said after that.

When Mom first went into her assisted living facility those of us out of town were on the phone with her all of the time. She got calls from across the country multiple times a day along with daily and weekly visits. I called her from the office often. But her hearing after a few years finally gave out and using the phone shortly thereafter became frustrating for her and us. Hearing aids so tiny were a chore they fell out and got misplaced. She didn't lack for care and attention, but the phone just became a futile exercise. Well now I'm stuck several states away and although visiting every few months that wasn't good enough for me or her. I wasn't going to stop communicating with her so in the meantime I began to write letters on note cards at least monthly.

She loved note cards and I have a drawer full of them because of her. Besides it was a great way to let her in on what we had been doing and to reminisce. When her eyesight started to fail my brother who lived up the road from her would read her the letters and sometimes her care providers would as well.

Mom raised five children and had a kaleidoscope of a life. She didn't miss a trick and the adventures are mind boggling including working at the shipyard during World War Two.

Being born in the 1920's and surviving until 2021 she lived through well everything. The depression, World War Two, Korea, Kennedy assassinations, Vietnam, the Big Band Era, Swing, Jazz, the British invasion, rock n roll the house was always filled with music from Mozart to Pink Floyd. She saw her "brood" become flower children in the 1960's and carpenters, professional ice skaters, teachers, and executives later in life. There was tragedy at home as well as loss success and prosperity. Through it all she navigated the lives of her children, her husband and friends with grace, dignity, and a whole lot of style and fun.

She had style to spare. She passed just shy of her 97th birthday. When we would ask how she was feeling she would say fine but "I'm suffering from too many birthdays." She was a pistol.

After she passed, her small box of letters, cards, and keepsakes that she had gathered in her room got mistakenly tossed out. I recalled when my sister died how comforting those letters were that poured in from friends, neighbors, and family. It was a jolt when she passed, and another one not to have those keepsakes that Mom had kept to help the healing process, so I began to write her again.

And why not write Mom again? Who's to say for sure she can't hear me as I'm writing? At bear minimum it was excellent therapy. Think art therapy meets psychic phenomenon. What you have before you are a years' worth of cards and letters. Mysteriously the urge for writing ceased a year to the date of her passing. Looking back, it was lucky to date the cards because how long she had passed, and the exact date had slipped my mind. I was gob smacked when the last letter was dated May 14th, 2022. But for some reason come June of that year I didn't feel the urge and isn't that like a mom? Get on with your life, I know you love me. But the last card written on May 14th gave me pause.

So why write this book aren't these memories personal? Well, I kept the cards in the hallway hutch, and I couldn't really mail them to her. So instead of them collecting dust I thought maybe sharing them might help someone or a lot of someones. With all the death our world has seen during this last pandemic each one of us has gone through some real stress, emotion, and loss. Our collective worlds have been rocked with unanticipated and despicably sad events.

 Talk to any healthcare worker, a nurse a doctor and the tales they tell and witnessed firsthand of family members unable to be by the bedside of their loved ones with their hands and faces pressed against windows will bring it home. Nurses having to hold the hands of the near deceased instead of family compounding the loss in a crippling way is devastating to all involved.

Real human contact is what fulfills us. We couldn't get to see Mom either, but those cards kept coming and those care providers stepped up to read them. We were lucky that there was a moment available to visit Mom again a few months before she died. She wanted to know where we had been and that broke our hearts.

Hopefully my experiences and thoughts will be relatable and maybe even comforting. Set aside the complexities and heart break of the pandemic who hasn't or won't be going through the process of seeing our parents grow old?

Dealing with hospitals, lawyers, insurance companies, assisted living facilities, nursing homes, and memory care just piles onto the emotion and stress already present in an aging loved one. It doesn't get more real than that. But more importantly I'm sharing these letters as a beacon of hope and faith and to celebrate Mom and her wisdom and to share that with you. Her voice and guidance I can still hear and rely on today and in this very moment. I'll say something and my wife will say "that sounds like Mimi." I can hear her voice from time to time and smelled her perfume in our house right after she passed. Besides it's nice to be nice. Yep, that's one of hers as well. So hopefully I captured some of all that if not the specifics, then at least the feeling in my correspondence. And that sharing them with you proves helpful, intriguing, and maybe even powerful.

May 23, 2021

To: Mrs. Jean DiMarco
Heaven For Sure Avenue Infinite Beyond Way
Universal, Universe ∞∞∞∞
From: You Know Who – Mr. Boo Boo

Dear Mom,

Well, it's been a week since you passed into the great beyond and what a show you gave Anne and I. It was so like you to wait until we finished our romantic night out and we were tucked into bed before you left. Thank you so much for playing "As Time Goes By" again for me, and you were right Vic Damone's version is sublime. I remember you and I watching Casablanca together the first time. I might have been ten at best. When Dooley Wilson began to sing you knew all the words and sang in such a beautiful voice. Casablanca has been and always will be my favorite. Watching it with you when it came on the television and later DVD was always a joy. And so, the very first thing I did after I learned you had passed was play the Vic Damone station on Pandora and wham there was our song. My whole body was numb and that was just the beginning. More to tell, more to say, more to write soon. We all love you, Mom.

Paul

<u>Readers Note</u>: Mom had a lifelong thing about the vocalist Vic Damone. I had no idea he did a version of "As Time Goes By" but recalled afterword that she had mentioned it to me a very long time ago. I wasn't even all the way out of the bed. In her honor I thought to play some Vic Damone. I had one foot on the floor as I brought up Pandora and I was stunned that song the first song on a never before played channel came up. My jaw was literally wide open. It wasn't sad I was feeling it was beyond that and rather a feeling of amazement that engulfed every fiber of my being that no mere mortal or happenstance could ever provoke.

June 1, 2021

To: Mrs. Jean DiMarco
∞∞∞ Infinity Way
Star Dust County
Universe, Universe
From: Paul

Dear Mom,

What a night it was on the 15th after playing our favorite song for me and way laying me out to the infinite reality the playlist kept on coming. "If Ever I Would Leave You" has quietly been one of my favorites but how would anyone know that as I kept that one to myself. And then "I'll Be Seeing You" by Frank. What a marvelous musical sendoff you gave me and Anne. As the night went on, we watched the new moon set. Anne noticed that it made a face with two bright stars high up in the night sky. The moon was a dark red and as it set, I told you Mr. Boo Boo says goodbye and a shooting star dropped through the heavens and the clouds. And if that wasn't enough the stereo that was still randomly streaming kicked off the famous NY, NY song – if I can make it there, I can make it anywhere – closing the show. What a great performance, light show and set list your send off to me was.

We love you, Jean. So much more to tell. I'll be seeing you.

Paul

<u>Readers Note</u>: Mom sung on the radio live as a child in the late 1920s and the love of music has been instilled in me since the day I was born. Camelot is another movie I recall seeing with my mother and the song "If Ever I Would Leave You" sung by Robert Goulet is the showstopper from that movie. Robert Goulet was another one of Mom's favorites and we actually ran into him at the Airport in the 1970's. Mom went up to introduce him to her two daughters. When the girls realized what was happening and still behind Mom's back one daughter took a hard right and the other hot footed it left leaving me standing there alone with my long 1970's hair in all my androgynous glory. Goulet laughed hard as Mom introduced her daughters and turned around to see only me. It was priceless. Mom took it in stride.

I'll Be Seeing You sung by Frank Sinatra also shook me to my core. Those lyrics in a moment like that come at you hard. "I'll be looking at the moon But I'll be seeing you" was emphatically on point wouldn't you say?

June 23, 2021

To: Best Mom Ever
Somewhere Out In The Universe
At Home with Poppie
Stella Avenue
Blue Moon Galaxy ∞∞∞∞∞∞∞
From: Still at the Beach- Atlantic Ocean – Planet Earth

Hi Mom,

It's a beautiful day in late June, mid 70's, and I thought of you. The windows are open, and the laundry is going. We are up and at 'em this morning. As you know after the light show and music mix the night you passed on Anne and I went to lunch the next day. Well, you don't need unearthly powers to figure that one out. We tried a new place on the water. Little neck steamed clams, a craft brew, a boat drink, and coconut shrimp is our version of heaven. A single mom and her four- or five-year-old son sat next to us and in short order delivered a message from heaven. Out of the blue he said," where's Mimi?" And his Mom said, "She's not here." There was a pause and he asked again, "Where's Mimi?" And the Mom answered, "She's with Poppie and they'll both be there when we get home." All of this took a few minutes on a quiet afternoon on a sun-drenched deck by the water with fishing boats and sail boats docked and floating by. Anne and I were both tuned in the whole way, and we were floored.

Thanks for the message, Mom. You always wanted us to call when we arrived home safely. So, we are more than grateful you dropped us a line. Give Poppie and the girls (all of them Wendy, Bevy, and your sisters) a big hug from us and we will see you soon – universally speaking- we still have things to do out here on Planet Earth. Feel free to see with my eyes, speak with my tongue and hear with my ears. Something I told your oldest daughter Jeana back in 1981.

Love,

Mr. Boo Boo

<u>Readers Note</u>: First off me and Anne headed out to lunch on a beautiful day by the water is no news to anyone, but I wanted to set the scene. Poppie is my dad who passed on six years earlier than Jean. My oldest sister Jeana passed away in 1981 at 26 years of age. Just married talking about children she thought Mom and Dad should be called Mimi and Poppie instead of grandma and granddad so after she had passed that's what we called them from then on.

July 17, 2021

To: Mom - Heaven
Somewhere with Jeana
From: Paul Back on Earth – Part One

Hi Mom

Hope all is well wherever you are. Dancing on a pin passing me in the hall, giving me a peck on my head while I sleep, hope all is very well. There is one other story from the morning after you passed. You sent us off with a magnificent light and sound show the night you passed (die is such a final word and doesn't jibe with the reality). And the next morning at lunch you let us know you and Poppie would be "home" when we got there. I hope you are not offended if we are not in a hurry still some things to accomplish down here. So, there we were finished lunch and decided to move to the Tiki bar by the water. We had a wide-ranging discussion with a woman of color about racism and politics and society as we listened to her tell her story. We had some laughs as well. When she said goodbye, a young couple sat down in her place. The young mother was very pregnant and due in August which made us raise an eyebrow. It was only an hour since we learned Mimi and Poppie would be "home" when we got there and so your birthday is in August, but you knew that. Anyway, we found out it was going to be a girl and yes, they picked out a name. When I heard the name divinity itself washed over me. A mixture of profound wonderment, enlightenment, tears of joy, bewilderment, and sadness my world was rocked when I heard the young mom say "Emily."

Jeana was thinking of naming her daughter Emily. I know this because big sister that she was she was interested in who I was dating. And at the time it was a little rowdy hippie girl named Emily. When Jeana heard that name she mentioned immediately, "Emily that would make a good name for a girl." She rolled the name around in her mouth with her husband's last name and I was honored. Hearing Emily's name at that moment let me know loud and clear that Jeana had you in heaven and without a doubt was there to receive you.

Lucky You,

Love Paul

Readers Note: This was a one-on-one conversation I had with Jeana about the name Emily in front of the house one summer day. I don't think she had a chance to share that with anyone before she died. Mom never spoke of it, and I know they were discussing names. That moment pierced my very soul.

July 17, 2021

To: Mom – Heaven
Somewhere with Jeana
From: Paul Back on Earth – Part Two

Hi Mom,

Wow two letters in one day. There was more I wanted to say about "Emily." It's not a name I hear very often these days. That morning Jeana, and I discussed the potential name of her hoped for child is a strong memory of blue skies and clean salt ocean air. It's not a faded memory and made more profound to me by Jeana's passing shortly thereafter.

Mom what a dynamite big sister/mentor Jeana was. The difference in our age made me look up to her and listen closely when she spoke to me about her experiences, her advice, her candor, her fun, her laugh, her mischief, her music, or a song I was learning she liked. We had a few misadventures together that are not faded memories and she always made me feel validated as a real person human being equal no matter how old I was or our age difference. Your daughter Jeana "got it" so to speak. The "Emily" moment with her so many years ago was so private and profound that without a doubt when the young Mom pronounced the name I was shaken or wakened to my core. Emily is such a rare name to my ears in 2021 in the mid-Atlantic there was no doubt, and my faith was reaffirmed and enunciated for the third time in less than twenty-four hours. It's been over two months since you passed and with all the music in my life you would think I would have heard Vic Damone's version of "As Time Goes By" it's not like I haven't tried to randomly pull it up again, but I have not and that is something in and of itself amazing.

Keep piercing my consciousness. See you when we get home.

Love,

Paul

<u>Readers Note</u>: In the span of fourteen hours with eight hours of sleep in between all of those coincidences just kept piling up on us. You can write them off as coincidences if you want that is your choice and why you were given a brain and free will. But the way they piled up on us like air traffic control gone amok was too big to ignore. The deep personal references seemingly buried in history that kept getting pulled out of me in an instant and underlined and enunciated with actual tactile events going on around us was a hotline to heaven or whatever you want to call it and I had to get it down in writing. *As Time Goes By, If Ever I Would Leave You, I'll Be Seeing You*, shooting stars and smiling moons, Mimi and Poppie will be there when we get home, and Emily

with her birthday in August all within a night and day. Wow! I mean how can you not get it when it's hammering your head like that?

August 13, 2021

To: Mom - All Around Us
Everywhere- Here and There
From: Us – Back on Earth – Part One

Dear Mom

A lot has been happening the past few days. First off happy birthday to you and what a birthday celebration you threw for us. It was an incredibly special day. At 9:30 am we were at a small, secluded park having doughnuts and coffee. It was Caid's 6th birthday. Moms and Dads along with several adorable well-behaved children ran the playground. There were only one or two melt downs and quiet corrections needed. I could go on about the adorable kids and young parents, Lucy's curly hair, Connors confident precociousness, Emma's saint like patience, and Annie's quips from a four-year-old hilariously salty like some senior who has seen and done it all. From that wonderfulness our 92-year-old Norwegian neighbor next door taught a language and cultural class. Anne learned a few phrases in Norwegian and baked a traditional Norwegian Almond Cake. You would love this along with a little coffee and a splash of Kalua. That night after dinner Caid and his brother Callum surprised us and came over with their parents and joined us under the screened in tent on the deck. What wonderful company they are both fun, calm, good story tellers and always laughter. We launched small fireworks into the air with much fanfare as the day drew to a close and our outdoor lights sparkled in the cool evening air. The next morning, we woke and realized it had been your birthday as well. But it was you who provided the perfect day for us.

Love,

Paul

Readers Note: Mom set an excellent example of who she chose to spend time with. She did not suffer fools and surrounded herself with good people. It's not always easy to do. You have to be mindful who you spend time with and why. And the neighborhood was always a source of friendship and fun. Mom and dad both had the welcome mat out and all walks of people came by and fraternized. With five kids there were a slew of roustabouts running around. Mom would sit the neighborhood kids down for lunch in our little nook and then off on afternoon adventures we would run. Bikes would be strewn across the side yard and then in the evening the adults would have their fun. We've tried to capture that neighborhood feel in our neck of the woods. It's not as easy as it should be, but when it comes together naturally the neighborhood lights up and comes together with positivity and isn't that the way we all want to live. Count your blessings if that's your routine but sadly it's not that way everywhere. But we have to keep trying it's what makes life worth living.

August 13, 2021

To: Mom
The Best
In My Corner
From: Paul – Part Two

Dear Mom,

Wow what a birthday treat, thanks again! For us it was the perfect day. So, what else… we finally found a quality handyman and tightened the house back just the way you and dad always kept our home together. The apple doesn't fall far from the tree. Little jobs become bigger jobs so get to them early and save some money. However, the big news is that my health is in great shape. Not just the house and yard but my health. Mom if you didn't stress health to me every day, I might have let that slide. I know how much you kept track of that, and all my numbers were good. So many sick people but brave going through chemo and losing limbs to Sarcoma. If I hadn't been on top of it, I might not be writing this right now. Rise to the challenge don't avoid that's what you taught us just by being you. Smart, calm, fun loving, loving loving, kind and as you used to say to me "it's nice to be nice." No one could have had a better Mom than you thanks for setting the example and quietly pointing the way to a successful life.

You and dad let me run down a few blind alleys until I saw the handwriting on the wall, but you kept me from going over the edge.

Love,

Paul

<u>Readers Note</u>: Just shy of ten years ago I was diagnosed with a one in a million cancers. Everyone thought it was something else a hernia no big deal. And I might have let it go but I watched it and knew something wasn't right. Let me tell you I caught it just in time as the damn thing was beginning to morph. Needless to say, we've eliminated as many toxins from our life and use vinegar to kill weeds as an example. Get regular checkups. Treat your body like you would treat your car or your home and "listen to your body" yep one of Mom's as well.

September 6, 2021

To: Mimi
Here and There Avenue - In Real Time Way
Manifested Reality -The Universe is Everything
Milky Way Road - Heaven and Earth 100810 102214
From: Paul – You Know Where and How to Reach Me

Dear Mom,

Well, it's labor day Jean and what a fun day we had with the neighbors. Anne and I hosted our monthly block party. We set up the tent and amplifier and the guitar and performed a two-hour set. Music really does bring people together and creates a little magic. Speaking of which thank you for visiting me a week or so ago. Anne and I had just finished entertaining one of her mom's old friends and we had the Tony Bennett station on, and all of those American Songbook classics provided the dinner music. Anne's Mom couldn't attend so we stepped in to show her friend how we roll. She stayed all night and hugs all around at the end of the evening. She lives alone and lost her husband a few years back. And so, we did an authentic kindness and had fun. Like you said, "it's nice to be nice."

That night I awoke to an overwhelming sent of perfume. I didn't recall any from our dinner guest or from when we embraced to say goodnight and Anne doesn't wear any. So, I awoke trying to identify the source smelling pillows and clothes and couldn't find any. Eventually I fell back asleep but awoke later with the same sent. It was such a mystery I asked Anne in the morning, and she confirmed Susanne wasn't wearing any. It was at that moment I remembered sending you perfume on two different occasions. Sure, enough when I searched my order list there was Oscar de la Renta from 2010 and 2014 so of course I reordered some more. When it got to the house, I immediately opened it and yep that was the unmistakable scent you peppered me with the night before. Wow mom you already have strong powers. Well, you were already so strong with all the tragedies thrown your way. Thanks for visiting me and giving us a nod for doing the right thing and showing a kindness to a friend.

Love,

Paul

Readers Note: When Covid hit, and we saw the Italians playing music from their balconies it struck me that we could do the same thing on our street. So unannounced to anyone I rolled out to the front yard and set up my modest rig and threw a concert. Doors opened up and soon there were families and children and cars pulling over. It became a thing. We started out doing it weekly and then bi-weekly and finally monthly until this summer. We threw the last one on July fourth. It may become a holiday event going forward now that the worst of the pandemic is over. But in any event, I will tell you in the midst of all that sadness and weirdness the music did its trick. The perfume thing is just bizarre in a good way.

October 12, 2021

To: Mom
From: Paul

Dear Mom,

We finally scattered your ashes in our garden and off of the pier. There were twenty people there to say goodbye and all of them were your children, grandchildren, great grandchildren, and spouses. We remembered how you loved us, took care of us, talked to us, and taught us. Many years ago, I asked you why everyone said our family was so special and I mean everyone from neighbors to business associates, cousins, friends, my friends, your friends…everyone. It was kind of weird, but you said without blinking an eye that it was because we loved each other warts and all. That is the lesson right there. Unconditional love.

We were given our own head to grow and find our way and it was only when we were headed down a dead-end road that you reminded us that was the wrong way to go.

Your five children were all different, but you saw the good and accentuated the positive in all of us and taught us how to live, love and have fun. And although there were a few tears when we stood at the pier for a random fisherman to take our picture every face from young to old was beaming with a smile.

A perfect family portrait which my dear you painted on all of our faces and left for us.

Love,

Mr. Boo Boo your Paul

<u>Readers Note</u>: That's what she called me "Mr. Boo Boo" she was always putting a Band-Aid on my knee or pulling a splinter out of my foot. She also had another expression when we were little and went out to play, she would say "don't blow away" in a little sing song voice. Recalling that right now puts a lump in my throat. What a wonderful human being she was.

Mom and part of her brood

Loving dad

Out on the Town Having Fun

I look a little concerned but Mom and big brother seem to be amused

Mom with her first two boys

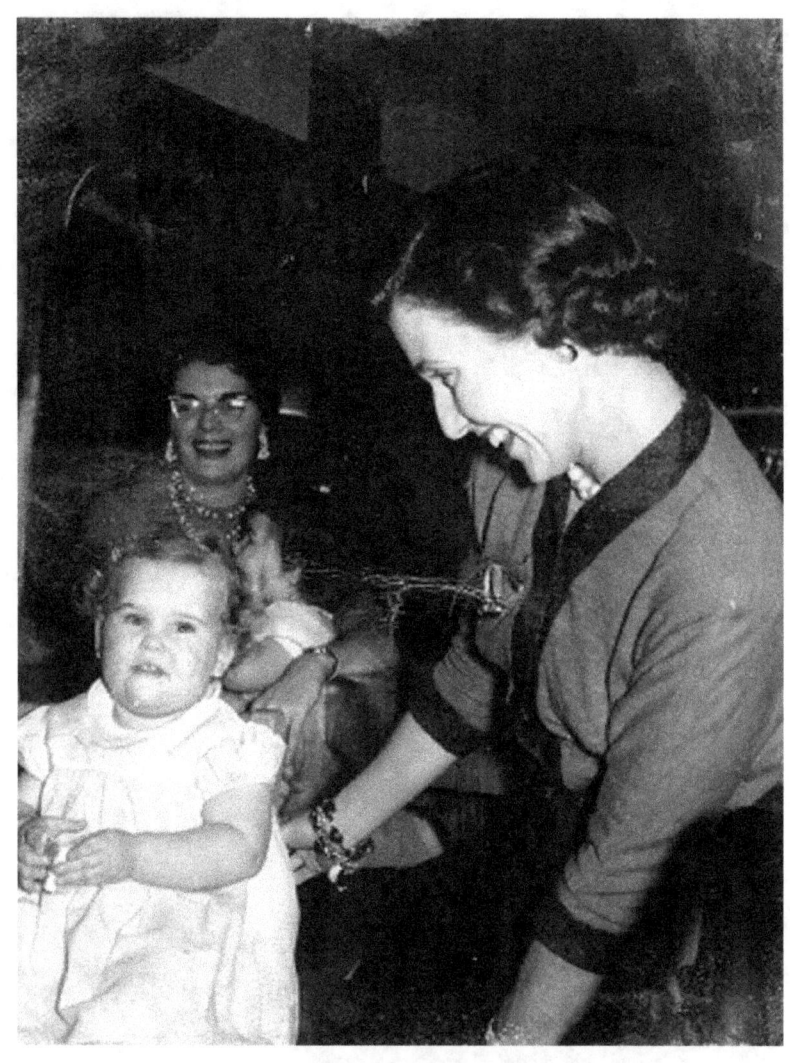

Mom with her oldest daughter. I love the way she looks at her children

Mom with her second daughter. Same look of love

Always Glamorous

November 1, 2021

To: Mom
Through the Space Portal Above
Looking Glass Lane
Out There Somewhere xxooxx
From: Paul
Back at Home

Dear Mom,

Well, what a surprise to see you the other night in my dreams. Face time with heaven was amazing. Literally there was a screen you and I were both looking at and the look on your face when you saw me was priceless. The dream began with Anne and I at home trying to fix a large digital screen. There was a portal floating above our house, ring shaped with black ops guys walking around it. Back in the living room Anne was tracing the wiring behind the sofa. In the brick fireplace there were tuning forks and large metal spoons attached to the grate. And of course, we were trying to work the remote control. At first a blurry picture started to appear. It was Amy in a Halloween costume and then bang your face from when you were in your mid-forties. When you saw it was me looking back at you your jaw dropped. Pretty fun huh? I guess there are surprises in heaven as well.

Back in regular time here on Earth, all is well. The whole family got together a few weeks ago as you know to scatter your ashes but honestly Mom, the

Pope, the President and all the dignitaries in the world couldn't come close to honoring you enough.

Love,

Paul

<u>Readers Note</u>: My sister Amy absolutely loved Halloween. Unfortunately, she was the second daughter Mom lost and four months after Dad passed. It wasn't all sunshine for Mom, but she was a soldier and her spirit indomitable. Anyway, that was a hoot of a dream and suitable for a Men in Black reboot. What a great woman.

December 1, 2021

To: Mom
From: Morning Time

Hi Mom,

Well, I'm in such a tremendous frame of mind thanks to you. Seriously all the wisdom, kindness, smarts and love you poured into me is just brimming. It's such a beautiful sunny morning and as we know you always loved the morning. Can you believe the kid you couldn't get out of bed can't wait to get up and enjoy the quiet solitude a bright beautiful morning brings. It's just another gift you have given to me that will stay with me always.

I remember the milkman who used to come to the side kitchen door. I may have been young, but it was awesome watching the two of you flirt with each other. He was a fit handsome fellow who obviously worked the land and the fresh milk and eggs. It was like something out of a movie. Me there at the kitchen table, you with your apron on, and he with his handsome face, short haircut and white overalls. Watching you in those moments I got a glimpse of the girl dad must have fallen in love with and to this day we still have our milk delivered. And every week when I go out to retrieve the old-fashioned glass bottles, I think of you and that lovely gentleman and how wonderful and perfect the moments of a morning bring.

What a wonderful thing it was to be a part of your life and a witness to all that was you and the world you created for us.

Love,

Paul

Readers Note: The milkman was a sweet guy. Bruce or William I cannot remember his name but do remember knowing it and everyone being on a first name basis. And he was kind to me the little toe head around Mom's apron. When he got leukemia and still delivered the milk with the obvious infection showing on his face and arms Mom was as sweet and loving as always. I remember them talking on the patio out of ear shot, she touching his arm. Then after he left Mom leaning up against the kitchen pantry sad shedding a tear with her back to me. In the moment I only could see his face and skin and not really have grasped all the details. Mom held it together until after he returned to his truck. Her grief was real, and I felt it as well. I did get an explanation in general and could see he was sick. But what sticks out in my mind in the quiet of the mid-day morning are the hushed voices outside the kitchen door the blue sky and everything bathed in sunlight and the intimacy of the moment as Mom and her milk man friend conversed and the way she touched his arm.

January 8, 2022

To: Mom
Sailing the Back Bay of Time
With the Wind to Her Back
From: Me – Spinning on Earth

Dear Mom,

Happy New Year. What a crazy time we live in but when I reflect on your time it's plain to see the times are always interesting. Doesn't matter what time it is, what the weather may be, the latest dance craze, fashion, or politics it's all a whirlwind of circumstance sometimes awful horrible sad other times happy and glad. And for some mostly in between. The ups and downs of this life, any life, any time seem remarkably consistent and so how someone deals with them defines not only the person but their surroundings.

Thank god you gave me the tools to cope. Your quiet dignity, your joyful smile, your focus, your playfulness, your genuine warmth for those around you and your smarts well if just a quarter of that rubbed off on me what a lucky person am I. Between you and dad you both gave me so many tools to make it through the constant struggle that life can be. "Be honest with yourself" may seem like a small thing to say but it is a fundamental building block to a successful life. It's "nice to be nice" and you are so right Mom. And it doesn't mean you are weak. In fact, it takes a tower of strength to do the right things. Honesty, integrity, class, and gratitude are a winning combination. No matter what this New Year brings I have the tools in myself to handle anything. You taught me how to act Mom. You taught me how to love Mom and you knew in real time what it means to be a parent. Like tending to flowers in the garden, some pruning, lots of natural fertilizer, plenty of water but not too much and sunshine and shade when needed. How proud you and dad must have been when we grew into the wind and stood straight and tall. Every one of us in a row with our own personalities, hopes, thoughts and ambitions and more than able to get where we wanted to go like the wind on the water you both taught us to sail.

Love,

Paul

February 3, 2022

To: Mom
Winter Wonderland
From: Me

Well Mom,

That was a heck of a January. Living this close to the coast we got a blast of snow two weeks in a row. It actually made for some magical times as both snow falls occurred at night. We went across the street to the neighbor's house and watched the snow with their little family. They have two young ones, and their parents are such delightful smart and accomplished people. Mom, you gave me an appreciation for that and watching their boys get excited about the snowfall reminded me of our winters back home. How we would get all bundled up in our snow suits and the old metal clasps of our snowshoes. And off we went across the street to the big hill behind the school. Sledding on our Radio Flyers and those old aluminum discs and inner tubes, anything we could get our hands on. But the best part was coming home to a roaring fire peeling of our snow suits and those galoshes. You waiting by the door to help your little frost-bitten peeps with their red faces and runny noses out of their soaked clothes. Wrapping us up in big fluffy towels to sit in front of the fireplace with hot chocolate with little marshmallows floating in them.

It was a slice of heaven and boy did we get some big snowstorms in those days. But what made it all so special besides flying down a hill at the old school was coming home to you. The joyous commotion of the five of us stumbling loudly back into the house with excited voices, exhausted, drenched and victorious in our pursuits only to be greeted by outstretched arms of love and care and happiness. It must have been beautiful mayhem corralling us setting us down in front of the big old fireplace to warm our bones. Sure, felt like heaven to me.

Love you, Mom.

<u>Readers Note</u>: It occurred to me while typing this she was also trying to keep us off the nice furniture and get all the boots lined up by the door and clothes down to the cellar, so we didn't destroy her house. But hey, she did it with a smile and love in her heart. She was a smart cookie as they said back in the day.

February 18, 2022

To: Mom
Old York Road Skating Club in the Sky
From: Me Dust Bowl

Dear Mom,

Happy Valentine's Day, well a few days late but you were never one to complain. Not that there wasn't something to complain about with five children spanning over twelve years. I remember one afternoon when Amy and I were spitting jello at each other having a great old passive aggressive ball. You finally sent us to our rooms with the wait until your father gets home threat. We deserved it. Dad coming from an abusive family that included stabbings at the dinner table had vowed never to strike his children. Trying to get our attention he faked slapped us across our faces and we burst out laughing something we ate, I guess.

Mortified, dad shushed us and then talked to us explaining we were all in trouble if we didn't get our acts together. Aligned with dad in getting him and ourselves out of the doghouse we sober upped pretty quickly. We loved you Mom, but it took an honest approach from dad to get us back in touch with our appreciation and then apologize. I wondered later did he confide in you his ruse gone awry attempt at being a physical disciplinarian and that we burst out laughing at his bluff. I hoped you two got a laugh out of that. It must have been like living with the Marx Brothers when the five of us all got going. But your level of patience was herculean as that stupid lacrosse ball banged against the side of the house. I'm still sorry about that and the skating rink.

Both of your girls could and loved to skate but me your youngest was having none of it as I was the worst hockey player ever to lace them up. Even the handicapped kid skated better than me. All those cute girls and I was too dumb to put it together, but laser focused on the candy machine…. "Mom, mom, mom can I have a quarter" in your face while you're trying to watch your girls skate.

I actually woke you up in the assisted living facility one afternoon as Anne and I had been sitting with you for a half hour watching you sleep. We had driven a long way hours on the road so I finally had to resort to desperate measures. Yes, we tried gently waking you calling out your name and sat patiently reading the newspaper and watching the news waiting but to no avail. So, I leaned over close to your ear and said the magic apparently triggering words, "Mom, mom, mom …I need a quarter for a Nestles Crunch bar." Your eyes popped open immediately and you slowly turned to look at me in a mix of horror, surprise, recognition and then a laugh. The patience of a saint.

Your skating coach Frank yelled at me "go away kid" and chased me away as I followed you around the rink while you were trying to take your lessons. Nevada, the office manager, locked me in the office with her and said leave your mother alone. Man, why didn't you all just use twenty rolls of hockey tape and tape me to the rails along the boards?

So, I'm sure your fine with a late card after all you have been through and persevered and realize all your patience and love has paid off. Yes, this relentless child of yours has been cleaning the house top to bottom the past few days including the windows because that's how you kept the nest clean for us and by now for me it's second nature. I wouldn't have it any other way.

Love you Mom,

<u>Readers Notes</u>: Growing up in the late 1920's and 1930's dad's generation beat the hell out of each other. Having a fist fight on a Saturday night was routine. Grandpa was an old-world terror and actually stabbed the back of one of his son's hands with a fork when he reached for the butter without asking. Dad and his brothers all shared the same room and slept in the same bed. His mother died in childbirth with his unborn sister when he was young. That generation went to work when they finished eighth grade. It was a different time and we have evolved like we are supposed to but those were dark

times. Harsh as it was when he grew up and met Mom, they wanted to build a better family life for themselves and their children, and they did. Mom graduated from high school and learned Latin but also remembers times that were so tough the trains carrying coal through the city would slow down going through the neighborhoods. The children could then climb aboard and kick the coal off the trains to the people waiting below. That's how they heated their homes.

My parents came of age during the depression. The upside-down world if you will and that informed their decisions, attitudes, and drive to provide the best for us leading by example with independent and critical thinking and sending us to good schools. They gave us an appreciation for art, music, culture, hard work and outdoor activities and that has been and is being carried down to the next generation of grandchildren. They did a great job and had a ton of fun along the way, and I love being the sum of both of them.

March 6, 2022

To: Mom - Within and Without -Here and There
Now and Then
From: Me

Dear Mom,

Well spring is on its way. The Maple trees are starting to bloom, and your boy was spreading mulch all over the flower beds. Not only do I find myself repeating the good example that you and dad set but I find myself repeating your iconic words. What a wonder that is to me on so many levels. How it comes so naturally and in contrast to my rebel without a cause teenage years. I guess we all go through that but luckily you were patient with me, and I finally saw the handwriting on the wall. It's a phenomenon that at the right time when the correct words are needed, I hear you speaking through me. Not only do I sound smarter than I am, but wiser. Those words of yours that come tumbling out of my mouth do the job help the moment and inform the listener and myself as well. The most amazing thing is that it brings me closer to you. I can literally feel you within me. The warmth is real and the closeness palpable. What a gift your patience, wisdom, thoughts, deeds, and words are and how they now bring you closer to me as if you are still here. And how when I think of you and those I love the sun always seems to come out from behind the clouds. How lucky I am to have found my way into your family and to be your son.

Love You Mom and Thank you,

Paul

<u>Readers Notes</u>: As I hear their words both Mom and Dad come out of my mouth, I'm like wait how did they get in the room. It happens at the oddest of moments usually important ones and there they are either one of them and it's my mouth moving. What a delight and it feels awesome as I'm like *take that* to an adversary or *how about that* to a loved one. What a power what a skill and it always leaves me in awe in the moment and afterwards as to what the heck is really going on around here and this existence of ours.

April 4, 2002

To: Mom in the Spring
From: The Red Cardinal in the Oleander

Dear Mom,

The azaleas are budding, and the forsythia is coming up. Yes, Spring is in bloom. Last week we were able to get together with the family back home. The old inn where we stayed was on point. We all missed you but remarkably our servers name was yours. Just your way of letting us know you were with us and a nod so it seemed you were giving us for getting and staying together. It's uncanny how I carry you with me. You never seem far away. How powerful love must be to be able to bridge that gap, that divide of time and space.

We had the ladies over for dinner last night. The youngest was seventy-five and the oldest ninety-two. It was the oldest who brimmed with life, health and warmth and the word you used to say to me all of the time "gratitude." A gratitude for the very smallest things in life like the azaleas and the forsythia and understanding how very large they are and the memories they bring. I can see the row of forsythia eight feet high running the full length of the house along the retaining wall. And instantly I get that feeling of home you created and remember your quiet wisdom, strength, patience, and love. I am a better man for it all.

Paul

<u>Readers Note</u>: The forsythia really was amazing and at least eight to ten feet tall. I remember trying to trim it back. It was a bear especially for a gangly teen to wrestle with. But dad and I would get the clippers out and the row grew full and tall. It was visible from inside the house but magnificent as you approached. Every Spring it would bloom sun yellow and your whole soul would light up from within knowing Spring was here and the warm weather was on its way.

Our home was surrounded by tall, shade trees. Azaleas in the front blooming in unison and the shade cooling the back of the house. Throwing those back windows open and hearing those blue jays call was magical. The creek was just a bike ride away where you could wander down to the water and hear the babbling brook cascade over the stone. I'm still drawn to the water, creeks, brooks, rivers and waterfalls and the sound of the constantly crashing waves on the beach. We aren't the ones with the boom boxes on the beach. We are the ones listening to the children playing, the gulls laughing and the waves splashing. Listening, thank you for that skill.

May 14, 2022

To: Here There and Everywhere
From: Home

Dear Mom,

What a wonderful trip we had down to Savannah. We jumped into the car May first and we are just back today. Savannah has a lot of history with the city squares giving it a small-town feel. Of course, we went to the Jepson Center at the Telfair Museum. You instilled an appreciation for art, history and culture a long time ago when you took us to the museum to see the Vincent van Gogh exhibit back in the early 1970s. I can recall clearly the roped off lines and staring deep into his sunflowers. Oh yeah, I may have just been ten years old, but I got it and the impact is still fresh in my memory. I can recall that moment clearly. It's up on speed dial in the old brain bank. I remember my big brother having to finally break my concentration so the people the throng of people behind us along the rope line could have their turn. We all went through the exhibit single file, and I was hooked then. I could write pages on all the exquisite trips short and long we have enjoyed thanks to the love and appreciation of travel, art, history, music, and culture you gave to us. The sheer beauty, lessons, and enhancements of it all have always adorned our life. Thank you for leading the way.

That and those yummy cucumber sandwiches you and I shared on those hot summer afternoons while those ocean breezes luffed through the house. I distinctly remember me and you alone immersed in those moments of sunshine and happiness enjoying the simple pleasure of crisp thinly sliced cucumbers and that special dressing you concocted. The beauty of the quiet of the day with the birds in the background the occasional laughing gull the snap of a flag the beauty of it all we shared it together.

Thanks Mom,

Love Paul

Readers Notes: That's it there was nothing more to say I guess except thank you for providing a wonderful environment to grow up in and be around. As children we absorb everything the good the bad and the ugly but some of us cast off the negative and accentuate the positive. With all that happened in our lives, mom and dad never played the victim. Dad used to laugh at all the Oprah like talk shows because his abusive father used the belt on all his children. And all the boo hooing that sold advertising on the television would make him laugh. Mom and Dad were very conscious in the art of raising children. They knew that each child came preloaded with their own personalities like peas in a pod all different shapes and sizes. Anybody who is healthy enough can have a child. That's not the hard part or the issue. It's raising the child where the rubber hits the road. The apples don't fall far from the tree. And as trite as those old sayings may sound, they are still bedrock solid truths, and you best pay attention to them. Some classics we heard from Mom and Dad:

Everything in moderation

You can lead a horse to water, but you can't make it drink

That's yesterday's newspaper

It's nice to be nice

You can't put a tuxedo on a jackass

Actions Speak Louder Than Words

If you are in a hurry and you make a mistake, how are you going to have time to fix it

If you have one foot in yesterday and one in tomorrow, you're pooping all over today

Don't look a gift horse in the mouth

Business before pleasure

House Devil Street Angel

House Angel Street Devil

Do unto others as you would have them do unto you

Live and let live

You can't shine poop

If it ain't broke don't fix it

Hard work brings good luck

A job well done is its own reward

The jobs not over until you clean it up

You work hard you play hard

The family that plays together stays together

It's called wisdom so if you are going to be a parent guard your thoughts, words and actions and set the example because your little ones are watching. They will emulate every nook and cranny of your very being. If you're selfish you raise selfish children, if you are boorish the same, if you are a bully ditto. Anybody can be a jerk. It takes real toughness and thoughtfulness to be kind. Mom and Dad were not perfect but if you're raised to think for yourself you can learn from the mistakes of those around you and follow the successful patterns of those you understand to be successful.

Mom and Dad both knew it wasn't just them who raised us but our surroundings as well. Siblings were taught to have a responsibility to each other. They brought interesting, creative, fun, smart, professional, good, hard working, and great people into our lives. They weren't all saints, plenty of interesting characters provided street smarts but all and all everyone's behavior, and example were as much of a road sign as those proverbial sayings.

Mom and Dad spoke up when we were out of line with each other and with ourselves. They pulled wisdom from the salt of the earth whether it was old sailors, boat builders, fishermen, laborers, or executives and the well-to-do. They surrounded us with excellent people and gave us a taste of the good life so we would want that for ourselves.

We were taught to value hard work. When I went to work as an adult my boss who was a luminary in the town told my father one night when they ran into each other at dinner, "if I had a son, I would want him to be exactly like Paul." I didn't give that moment to Dad. Dad and Mom gave that moment to each other. I am just a reflection of who and what they are and how they meant to be. Sure, I bring myself to the table every day but the decisions they made and the examples they set inform who I am.

Dad and I would work side by side in the hot sun bagging leaf clippings, trimming back shrubs, climbing the roof of the house together to wash the roof before power washing became a thing. One day when we were up there the chief of police drove by wound down his window and hollered up at us "I'm not messing around with you two guys." Dad had me under the house as a kid crawling from one side to the other in the dark turning on water mains putting up insulation. We swung hammers together fixed bikes and scrapped the weeds out between the joints in the sidewalk and driveway (before poisons like Roundup). These days I use plain white distilled vinegar. When I moved into my new home the neighbors wanted to know who the hell I was, sweating and working the yard, sweeping the street, trimming the bushes, keeping the house inside and outside tight. I'm my parent's son that's who I am.

On those hot summer days we got at it early together and at lunch we would sit in the screened in porch. Mom brought us our lunch that she had prepared while we were working outside. In other words, she was working inside as well. Those lunches with the three of us together those beautiful blue skies and those lovely ocean breezes were a thing of quiet beauty. A few pretzels and a small pony bottle of beer and we were back at it for the afternoon. A job well done is its own reward. Know that live that and all will be well. The work over and the endorphins up we had fun with a jump in the water. Then off we would go to greet our nights, misadventures laughter and love. To this day when I come off the yard dripping in sweat a jump in the pool and then there is my beautiful bride with a beach towel and lunch and off we go to greet our nights with misadventures laughter and love.

Show your children the right way to live. You are their example. Show them how to work. There are no short cuts, and strange as it seems the easy way out is always harder in the long run. Show them how to play, laugh and love, not to hate. Don't waste time pretending. Confront the challenges head on and be honest with yourself. It's a small planet we all live on with a razor thin atmosphere so our responsibilities to each other are real. Every choice we make affects the foundation of our very existence one and all. Make successful healthy choices and your life and the lives of your children will be healthy and prosperous. It's a seemingly simple thing but it takes, strength, persistence, and consistence and besides "it's nice to be nice."

<u>Afterward</u>: The power of example cannot be overstated. For the most part good parents' equal good people. If you want to make a difference in this world how you raise those little strangers, you have invited into your home is everything. I'm not saying it's easy, but Mom and Dad should have written a book... so I did.

Mom

Mom Dad and Paul Power Trio

Mom and Mr. Boo Boo

The Notecards and Letters

Paul Burke DiMarco is the author of Journey Home by Paul Burke. Dear Mom - Letters to Heaven is his second book.

© 10/10/2022 Paul Burke DiMarco - All Rights Reserved

Don't Blow Away Press

www.ingramcontent.com/pod-product-compliance
Lightning Source LLC
Chambersburg PA
CBHW050247010526
44107CB00003B/225